Echoes, Shadows, and the Wind

Catherine Maia Santamaria

Copyright © 2023 by Catherine Maia Santamaria
All rights reserved.

Book cover photograph: Jose Santamaria
Book cover design and formatting assistance: Jose Santamaria and Dekie Hicks
Editors and proofreaders: Barbara Odom and Jose Santamaria

First Edition 2023

ISBN 978-1-7357604-8-3

Books may be ordered through your local bookstore or by visiting www.catsantamaria.com.

Wheredepony Press
Rome, GA 30165

Dedication

This book is dedicated to my husband, Jose,
Who makes everything worthwhile, and whose love adds brilliant
colours to my life.

Contents

Summer

Crystal Avenues	3
Dance Dream	4
Dust Rose	5
Butterfly	6
Borderlining	7
Sawdust Dreams	9
Blues Again	10
Luv Note Progressions	11
Some Sweet Mourning	15
Jungle Cat	16
Rainbow	17
In the Limelight	18
Such a Gypsy	19
For Cheechah's Dreams	21
Awhile	22

Autumn

Surfaces	25
Two Shells	27
Wildflower	28
Restless Blues	29
The Reception	30
The Deer	32
My Poetry Allowed	33
Collaboration	34
Through the Eons	35
I Wonder	41
Brother Blue	42
Volcano	43
Elusive Musings	44

Winter

Quarantine Blues	47
Illusion Confusion	48
Mean Morning	49
The Ice Carver	50
Shadow Woman	51
Looking Through the Glass	53
Surplus War	54
The Ultimate Disrespect	56
…tactics	57
Again and Again	61
Universal Voice	62
Velvet Black	63
Last Year	64
Exegesis	65
Thunder with the Snow	66

Spring

May's Lament	69
Wander Down the Road	71
Sun Bluems	72
Today	73
Silent Shadows	76
All the Smiles	77
Loving Stranger	78
Balance!	79
April 22nd at the Symphony	80
Listen to the Blues Done Right	82
Love Circled	83
Whistle Bird	85
Hot Sunlight	86
Exist	87

Acknowledgements

I have always written with the inspiration and critique of our various clowders of cats, so many, many purrs to them. Words will never be enough to thank my late parents, Mary and John, who instilled in me a lifelong appreciation for writing. So many friends have supported my writing: Amy, Ann, Aunt Marti, Barbara, Christina, Dave, Dekie, Fran, Jodi, Jose, Julie, Kathy, Lance and Sherri. From friendship to patience, from praise to nitpicking, from easing my blues to celebrating, these friends are/have been my writing village. So much love and so many thanks. Newer on my scene is the Rome Area Writers group, whose members offer writing companionship and assistance, and to whom I committed to the goal of publishing this book last year. Almost made it. Thank you for this community of writers. And our dogs? They never cared about writing, but always stood by me with their loyalty. With deepest gratitude to all and for this gift of writing.

Catherine Maia Santamaria

Summer
Dancing on the Sand

Catherine Maia Santamaria

Crystal Avenues

An opalescent dawn invites us
to wander together
along avenues of drusy crystals
that wend through lush vines and trees.
Sunlight and dewy flowers mingle in prisms.
Later, hot rain drenches the silver fronds and us,
draping the forest in humid perfume.
An amber sunset melts the day
and our paths flow to the beach
at last the salted wind from over the ocean
and silver stars from above cover us
in a midnight of sapphire blue.

Catherine Maia Santamaria

Dance Dream

I'll be your dream for this dance
for however long the music lasts.

Holding me, your touch so light
as if I'm a bird poised to fly …

The warmth of your stranger's arms
wrapping me close in your cloak of charms.

Your musky scent so unknown
yet welcoming as coming home …

Slowing, almost still with lust
Drifting 'midst the glitter and the dust …

I'll be your dream for this dance
for however long the music lasts.

If someday we meet again perchance
remembering fondly our brief past

with you thinking we could dream anew
I will say: "Ah! But I have already danced with you!"

Dust Rose

Dust rose
crumples
in her fist.
Now wafts
the musk
of last year's bloom.

Catherine Maia Santamaria

Butterfly

I saw
an umber brown black butterfly
with net lace wings long.
I turned to gaze the flight:
it flew past my blue gaze.
It flew into the searing white sunlight...

                    ...and past again.

Borderlining

This borderline has become a chasm
and I am falling
throughout our conversations
into your arms
that ask me to hold you
as a child, as a man,
as always and only I can.

I am falling
no holds barred
as we wrestle
with our questions
and our tears fall inside,
filling us even more wetly, drenching us,
with desire for more than we will ever have:
each other
and the place where there is no time,
no right and wrong,
only the rhythm of this song
and our dance.

Our bodies taut as though it were our last chance
and wet as we are
there is fire and no relief,
for once again we create a world
with a hell and no heaven
because we believe in another Heaven.

So sweet release comes only in the morning
when we are still virgin
and our world is not destroyed.

Come the night, I would see you again
and walk this borderline.

Sawdust Dreams

I was wont
    to wrap myself
in your words
but you only created
sawdust dreams:
dry,
    subject to change
        by the whims
        of the wind,
empty
    unfulfilled
        and scattered.

Catherine Maia Santamaria

Blues Again

I've got the blues again
    the lie down or cry blues
        the take flight or write blues
                        again...

Luv Note Progressions
and All That Ramblin' Jazz

It's hard to let go of something
you've never really had.
Take luv, for example.
If you've ever had a sample
you think it's everything.
You haven't got a clue
that what you thought you felt was true
was your imagining.

...

Stay with me tonight
take me in your arms
and hold me as a virgin
or love me as a woman
it's all the same to me
for where does meaning go
when I flow
into your arms?

...

Hold me yes so tight
until the night light shows
we are so much alike:
we toss and turn our fears

of one loss to another.
So stay with me tonight
until daylight breaks
us apart.

...

Your guitar strings mutely stare,
asking me do I truly dare?
What songs can I possibly share
just with you?

...

Black stars
in your eyes.
Where did the music go?
From where do the words flow
to soothe this poet's humble soul?
And two?
How far could two go
in your eyes?
Where did the time go?
What happened to the poetry?
Why don't you mind?
Writing
with thoughts too complex
to roam so aimlessly.
Blind as you think I am I see
all your cliches merely serve the lies
in your eyes.

...

My life is so many things
to no one but myself.
Yet you'd put it on a shelf
and file it away for future reference.
Have you even any preference
for the type of person
that you would marry
or bury
with(out) illusion
in your everyday confusion?

...

I feel as though I am standing upon a stage
in some Shakespearian play
speaking my soliloquy in an aside:
my declaration of love
heard, but not listened to,
as you rehearse your lines
and wait upon your cue.

...

Your love dropped away from me
like a sheltering robe
cloaking me,
wrapped about me so carefully,
and folded gently.
Then you pulled away your holding arms

and it draped the floor
in clouds of cloth,
leaving me
standing there,
barely standing.

...

Rain and word of you gone again.
Borrowing a cloak of grey steeled rain.
Braving this old weathered news: you're gone.
I'm silently stumbling through muddied love,
following hope's slowly drowning paths,
bracing myself 'gainst your bitter wind,
awaiting the light gliding swan of time.

...

Heart parts flown
and my blood flowed,
I am finally free of you.

Some Sweet Mourning

lay me down softly now
on the white warm sand
some sweet morning

let my blues wander
from life's roads to along the ocean
let my soul flow free

for the sea gulls call to me
and I travel the sleep dream
away ... away ... away ...

white turquoise water
mingles becomes angel rain
white green sea spray
rises flies to the rainbow

white blue light
melds fuses with the sun
and my soul flows fully free
some sweet mourning

Catherine Maia Santamaria

Jungle Cat

Like a jungle cat
        you stalked me,
baiting and waiting,
then you

    L
        E
            A
                P
                    E
                        D

upon me
with so much heat
    that I swore you did not love me,
it was only passion.
Then you said: "That is love, after a fashion."

Rainbow

luminescent blues (violet)
    fading
through to (ultimate) reds

  colouring the sand
      wetly to moist gold (shiny)

...tracing shadows of your name
      in the tangerine sand...

my hair cascading across you
    (wildly)
washed seaweed

 misty, dewy-eyed
     dripping drops of rain

a pool of iridescent bubbles
  popping, plopping
 (emerald) frogs

the zephyrs fly
   drifting (softly)...

blue, blue, bubbling deeply, shimmering blue

Catherine Maia Santamaria

Such a Gypsy

She'll be here until she goes
dancing easy, maybe slow.
Come watch the river flow
and see her as a gypsy.

She's a tumbleweed child
gone almost half-wild.
The winds of change do blow
wherever they will go,
and they can move her
in and out of time.

Don't tell her your name,
she couldn't bear the pain,
no not again and again.
Not when she is the gypsy.

She'll go and leave you fast
for vistas far more vast.
She doesn't want to see her past.
She'll be the first one gone
up in the morning, headed on
with the tide and her song.

Oh, do you want her?
You can never tell her.
Just stand by the river's edge,
knowing she's a gypsy.

   She doesn't want your words,
   just your laughter and your voice.
   She'll always make her choice.
   Whirl with her a while.

      If she ever hears you call
      and say you'd stay forever,
      such a long time forever,
      she will dance away.

         She'll be here until she goes
         dancing easy, maybe slow.
         Come watch the river flow
         and see her as a gypsy.

Catherine Maia Santamaria

In the Limelight

Bird
beat beat
dance/sway the feet
clap/clap the hands

flap flap
wings/beat the air
soar/catch the light

step step
can't/stop it now
hop/jump again

sweat sweat
quench/drink a drink
quick/leap the feet

turn turn
chance/speaker leap
shout/watch us prance

blur blur
cling/sing along
gold/dust the air

sweet sweet
embrace the heat
in the trance of
dance dance

For Cheechah's Dreams

ephalents lumber through purple woods
rhionsoberouses float
scarlet brids eat sweet pink cake
mockmees jump
jirrafffes munch on yummy-yum trees
zeebras prance
buzzy-bees dance through sunny flowers
carmels flump
fluffabos graze on hazy plains
kolollas loll
who-hoos peer through candy-cane branches
maflingos skate
flutter-bys skim over fluffy fields
and Cheechah smiles

Catherine Maia Santamaria

Awhile

The stone masons were unskilled
        when they carved this bridge.
The rock is hard, but flawed.

In need I come to you
  to walk over these cobbled streets,
ancient bridge,
       over trolls.

  The water wanders beneath,
      turning the wooden water wheel,
         stirring silken webs of spider netting.

I imagine over there in the green leaves and
    lavender hyacinths
we could sit and speak awhile.
   Whisper lest the elves be disturbed, elude.

Nestled soft against moss and bark
I can speak my sadness.

  Touch me quietly, gently,
      but hold me strong.

Autumn
Through-hiking Tangled Trails

Catherine Maia Santamaria

Surfaces

"Let me buy you a drink,"
      he smiled with a grin.
      Suddenly I found
      this stranger looking in
      to my past ready to sell
      me my tomorrows.

Without turning from my chair,
      "I don't drink," I said,
      "and it's hard to tell
      my future from my sorrows."

The place was quiet, for a change that is,
      and he sat down and downed a whiskey.
      After a round or two of winks and fizz
      he turned and gave me his house key.

"I won't keep house for any man," I said.
      "I'd gladly be your friend for a while,
      but if the pay is just to lay in your bed,
      I'm sorry, that's not my style."

The music came on and the guitarist was good
      or I would have left then and there.
      Then he leaned over and whispered:
      "You should reconsider my offer. It's fair."

I meet this man everywhere I go.
    He won't believe my retort of, "No.
    I'd rather spend nights alone without you
    than a lonely eternity living with you."

Two Shells

Two shells
of pale amber
glint in sifted sunlight,
only to be shattered by a
gull's cry,

as our
two thoughts of love
that formed so slowly and
imperceptibly were broken
by lies.

Water
reflecting this,
washed yet drowned the shells,
leaving marks on the sand and
our hearts.

Catherine Maia Santamaria

Wildflower

As I flirt with the delphiniums
    and dance with the dahlias
you are charmed,
    not seeing the harm in plucking me.

I'm a child of this garden gone wild.
I have grown with the sunflowers
    to kiss the birds in flight
I have cradled with the moon fog
    to while away the night.

I can't believe it when you say
    you'd put me in a vase
        to pretty up your place,
            to bring a smile to your face.

But I cannot leave this, my perfect place,
just for your whimsey
    for even with water and the dawn
not even you could save me.

Restless Blues

I've got
      those raw restless angry blues
      that make me want to use
           everyone I meet…

… 'til I meet you,
      yes, help me lose them
      in your hard hard heat
      'til sweat is sweet
           and I am forged anew.

Catherine Maia Santamaria

The Reception

Ah, what a lovely reception!

The veiled stares and sips of wine
and incidentally not much else at all,
just the requisite murmurs of slight politeness:
"My dear, the dress you are wearing is
    enchanting!"
and "Ooh, the hors d'oeuvres are simply divine!"

My words are lost as you cross the floor
and implore to hold me with(out) illusion,
in the fusion of musical notes and symbols
intermingled with thimbles of caviar.
Why are we trying to determine just who we are?

And so the dance continues
as a tangle of tangos with
you in the lead, me in the follow,
each step and stumble ringing more hollow.
Yet how can we stop?

For the music is ceaseless and endless,
a whirling waltz of pretty tunes
    and petty endearments
whispered into my perfumed ear.
At midnight shall we stop?

Or shall we go on,
playing and laying our games out,
arranging them spread-eagled on the bedlam,
    seeking pillows of comfort between sheets of deception?

Ah, wasn't that a lovely reception?

Catherine Maia Santamaria

The Deer

Your lips softly touched mine,
deep brown eyes gazed at blue,
and I was poised, flighty,
startled at the gentle suddenness of our meeting
on crossed paths in the woods.
Then, skittering, we left.
                                      Willow-gone.

My Poetry Allowed

Yes, I had to come tonight
      and listen to your blues.
I wanted to be one of the anonymous faces,
but you play in such intimate places!

Now, as my thoughts stray with your songs
      my heart is torn open.
As your melodies ask to be heard,
and I think of mingling them with my words.

But keep the spotlight from my face!
      This is your show
and if you see me watching you
you'll see tears and truth.

Oh, how I wanted to listen then leave
      but now I believe in you.
I would turn away my fears
and drink your beers
and read my poetry aloud to you.

      And my poetry allowed...

Catherine Maia Santamaria

Collaboration

How much would you give to me
      if I offered you all that I have?
      How much would you share?

Would you share your melodies with my words
      and not be amazed
      when their meanings changed?

Would you stand in the spotlight
      and hear the applause
      and acknowledge my muse in a pause?

After the groupies have come
      and had their fill
      of songs and words and time to kill,

after they've ripped your clothes
      would you believe that I am in tatters
      as you leave the stage?
Would we still go home together
      to fill pages and sheets with love?

Through the Eons

Street Lamp Shadows

Friend,
your echo comes
even as you said it would
in the echoes of time.

I stand beneath the street lamp
bathed in the yellow gaslight
with its pale green cellophane glow of reality
touching me.

Wind, blow windy, wind free,
free me.

Shadows faintly etched on the concrete
spread in different shades of brown and grey.
Yet it is still so still.
Blow windy, wind free.
My shadow moves,
bronze shadow,
shadow hair, softly blowing,
flowing, blowing.
Stirring, I pick a mimosa blossom,
later to give to you.
I lean against the street lamp
and sniff the bloom's sweet scent.

Catherine Maia Santamaria

It is so summer warm.

Windy, come wind.
Shivering and slightly laughing
with glad madness, I wait.

I drift further with the light,
light of warm yellow, cool silver,
the shades of a grey sky slightly
tinged still with a pale version of a sunset.

Now the wind blows,
caressing me,
mingling
the sweet scent of mimosa.
The shadows of our echoes,
the echoes of time,
the echoes, shadows and the wind.

Wind, blow windy, wind free,
fully free.

Brittle Wind

I stood beneath the street lamp again tonight
but I was numb.
The darkened sky still held colours,
but they were dull.

Echoes, Shadows, and the Wind

The wind blows,
freeing all the leaves to fall,
swirling them softly,
all around me,
yet not one touched me.

Friend,
I lost touch with you
so, I swallowed
the prerequisite six pomegranate seeds
and sank under deep snow
for a winter hibernation
of white and quinine.
Silence lasts
such a long time
in the cold,
quiet frost of winter.

Where I am
I hear no echoes
see no shadows
feel no wind
scent no mimosa

even silence once had echoes....

Ice
crystals form and
my mind,
hidden in hoarfrost,
will thaw only slowly.

And the wind will come
even the brittle wind
to blow to me, through me
to thrill me
stilling me,
chilling my soul
yet filling it.

Echoes in the Desert

Friend,
years ago, I came to this desert
deep in the canyons of time,
this alone place
so seemingly, unutterably barren
with wind storms of shadows and sand
where cacti
have white flowers that bloom
only every one hundred years,
and only at night.

You are the one who led me to my muse
through your poetry.

I wander here again now
seeking my muse, courting her,
currying her favor
and find you instead.

Thumbing through the past's pages
through the yellowed ages
hot dry wind,
aloneness and you pervade
my searching thoughts.

Shall I remain to tame
the unicorn of time
that ravages sweet memories
of innocent beginnings?
Or reject it as one more metaphor
cluttering up the landscape
of our brief poetic wanderings
in ageless canyons and caverns?

My muse, where does she go
when not with me?
She who flits from
place to place,
time to time.

With whom else does she rhyme?
Does she reside with you now?
And fleetingly flirtingly occasionally,
and oh, so teasingly and briefly
come to me?
Unfaithful, capricious
heartrending wench that she is.

So, she is here again
playing her hide-and-seek game.

Catherine Maia Santamaria

The wind begins to blow
my words stutter to flow.
And I know, oh, yes, I know
that through the eons,
She will come
and sometimes bring to me
unbidden,
thoughts of you,
ancient echoes,
swift shadows,
and scents of mimosa
carried by the wind.

I Wonder

I wonder how many walks I've taken
      thinking you were by my side.
I wonder how many hands I will have to hold,
      after our good-byes.
I wonder how often we were thinking
      of loving one another.
I wonder how long it will take
      to free ourselves for others.

I wonder how many broken branches
      I've picked up off the ground.
I wonder how many eagles I've seen
      flying free, unbound.
I wonder how many pieces of driftwood I've held
      and wished that I could keep.
I wonder how many I've had to throw away
      and then just sit and weep.

I wonder how long you've known me
      and why at first you cared.
I wonder how much love we've had
      that we've really shared.
And then I wonder when
      you were ever really there.
And then I wonder, where?

Catherine Maia Santamaria

Brother Blue

all I want to do is write
don't get me uptight
force me to show my hand
before I'm ready to
you'll just make me blue
there's no way to take it all in
and put it out again
in one big shout
make me feel down and out
had to refine all this with time
line it up with a rhyme
or two and a meter for measure
I don't write these sad songs
just for pleasure
say I don't have to hear
the music in my head
just take what I've got
and let it be said
yet there you go again
winding around my ink lines
and leaving signs
to my muse
oh brother
brother blue

Volcano

Fuming, foaming,
       tumultuously arising,
      violently violet,
deeply glowering crimson abyss,
         erupting.

Bursting forth in red orange colors,
  light silver vapor mists,
      cascading,
  pouring over, spilling.
   Heat and sudden gray change.
  Platinum showers
streaked with white gold ashes,
    still rushing ruin.

Everything now so clearly
                black and grey.

Catherine Maia Santamaria

Elusive Musings

Soft, soft…
   For years I have braved your bravado
   and borne your dreams.
   Listen now to the silence of a mother's womb
   before life arouses screams.

Curve, curve…
   I adventure almost everywhere:
   moon clouds, earth dirt, sea brine.
   Wander down paths that always lead home
   and let your footsteps fall in time with mine.

Flow, flow…
   Come peruse my elusive musings
   as they weave themselves into words,
   for when I've written, my soul is mute and breathless
   awaiting echoes or flights of freedom's birds.

Winter
Uneasy Hibernation

Catherine Maia Santamaria

Quarantine Blues

Recognizing the blues once again,
embracing their numbing caresses,
slipping under the covers
slipping as their lover.
Slipping …

Now who the hell are you, Anxiety,
with your jagged edges
keeping me awake
all night?
Never knowing which will come
the frantic or the numb.

I'll take the blues
but now my mind
won't let me have the choice.
Unmoored,
seeking connection with
anyone else.
Anyone?

Just let me sink down
into the loving comfort of my blues again.

Catherine Maia Santamaria

Illusion Confusion

Our past reflects who we are to be,
but I'm told we certainly can change.
This irony does so confuse me,
this, and memory's ability to rearrange.

How can we forget who we once were?
These mysteries are hard to explain.
It seems it's illusions we prefer,
for truth's eloquence seems far too plain.

Mean Morning

It was a mean morning,
    a raw morning,
a morning of frozen bones and witch's breath.

The time for warmth and
    snuggled slumbers was over.
    Those soft dreams one drifts with
    to be retrieved again at night
        were cut off neatly by daylight's scissors.
Alarmed awake.
Even the word hurt with difficult w's and cruel k's:
uh-wwwwaakkkkhh echoing with
    ache ache aches.

Outside,
sleet sheets covered the bed of pansies,
not even snow to ease the sharp landscape.
    Ice, slick and clear, slid around
    and into every crevice,
        splitting rock and root.

    Proclaiming stillness and detail,
throwing the land into relief without giving any,
    and mercilessly staying the same
        bitter, mean morning
                throughout the entire day.

Catherine Maia Santamaria

The Ice Carver

Shaping and molding your world first in tallow,
then burring and chipping shards of hard ice.
Using ethereal materials
to freeze time
for an instant
to celebrate an occasion
that is forgotten more quickly than the ice melts.
The occasion being more imperfect than the carving.

I watched you run from
country to country
woman to woman.
Then you came to me
and called me ice
your greatest compliment
arrowed straight from your artist's soul.

But when you tried to sculpt me
your creation was neither timeless
nor of me.
You turned away too soon and in disappointment,
for you never saw the amber essence of my heart.

Shadow Woman
and Singer of Songs

I can see from your face
      you are a Shadow Woman:
All of those lines of lies
      so innocently told to yourself.

You are always
      a reflection of him
      whomever he is this time.
Forever following
      in the footsteps of his whim
      thinking maybe you'll win this time.
You just can't win
      if you don't know
      the rules of the game.

The rules stay the same
      but the longer you play
      the higher the price you pay
      to learn them.

I can't help you
      and no man will
      but still:
      if you just shut your eyes
those one-way mirrors with real tears
      just shut your eyes to him

Catherine Maia Santamaria

      and listen to your voice
       it gives you every choice.
          Every chance,
        every dance
in the world is yours!

Looking Through the Glass

Looking
through the glass:
mirrors that must be read backwards
while running forward
and getting where now?

Under-
standing on one's head:
how often people demand one to be
standing up or
lying down!

Over-
looking in the window:
bewildered but still trying the door knob.
Why all the freedom and loneliness
outside?

Catherine Maia Santamaria

Surplus War

Leftover death
of a million heroes
who had nowhere to hide.

Filled shelves
with reminders
of un-lived lives from the past.

Buy someone's used backpack:
maybe he died from being stabbed in the back,
maybe by his own country.

Buy an unused gun
because the world still isn't right
in your mind.

The cost is measured in dollars,
never in hearts and truth.
For the pain would be too great and
morals are unaffordable.

Crates of debates
and caskets of hate.
The stories of war all told
with different versions for different times.

All those lies to make it right.
After all, God or Allah or whomever
you/they/we believe in
is on <u>our</u> side
and you must be ready
to die to prove it.

All that pain wasted.
All those wasted heroes.
All those heroes lost.
All of us lost.

Men and women came back with nightmares
broken and confused, but (un)lucky? to be alive.
We have our nightmares at home too,
Knowing so many lives are held in other peoples' plans,
and your hands, your courageous, trembling hands.

Catherine Maia Santamaria

The Ultimate Disrespect

We cheer you on when you leave to serve,
young and whole and strong.
You give your youth, your dreams, your limbs,
your hearts, your souls, and your minds.
You come back pieced together
by your fellow soldiers,
yet oh so broken, some far beyond repair.
We give you a hearty handshake upon your return
And say "Thank you for your service,"
your country doesn't help you
with the fervor that it sent you
and most of us just don't have a clue
though we try….
And when you die,
sometimes we mourn you as hometown heroes,
and cover you in our flag.
Sometimes we show the ultimate disrespect,
and leave you in the funeral home
with no one to pay your body's rest.

...tactics

drawn circles
      that debate
the plausibility of it
    feasibility
    probability
swing around with imprecise gyrations
      outlined in black etched anxiety
blandness facing the outside of it
              around
              afloat
outpouring of blasphemies
sourly awakening
quietly reassuring all propositions concerning it
    reaffirming
    publicizing
disconcerting ideals that were understated
      at one small glance
vaporize
releasing plastic straw dart guns
      aimed at total rehabilitation
of government religion and love

              ... it
              ... it
              ... I'm
lying always lying down
bleeding always bleeding redly
dying always dying noiselessly

quietly filing through it
      filtering
      faltering
vaguely bringing back a torn shirt
that had a pattern of peace carved in the back
      slaking thirst in the water
near the base of a thorn bush's roots
spawning low morality
          and mortality
          not normality

back there
      craving respite
rapid movements of mouths and hands
flail to find ways of handling it
         dealing
         interrelating
realization of failure does not disturb
the makers of it
    takers
    fakers
                       ... of
                       ... of
                       ... or
                       ... oh
quoting never quoting accurately
bartering never bartering enough
yawning ever yawning ceaselessly
peace that was thrown away by a paper doll
      all because the accusations seemed so appropriate

      … at the time
succinct statements
      crumble easily when scrutinized
by those who seek structures in it
                    of
                    on
mutability
      saturations
      inspiration
      limitation
      concentration
      creation
tangible variations invert the causes of it
                    losses
                    flaws
arrogance arranges all the implications of it
                    stipulations
                    manipulations
vibrantly calling to the supplicants of it
                    supporters
                    sufferers
fashioning influential apologies
the mindless affluence
      of establishments
arousing absoluteness

bringing no alleviation to it
      mediation
      meditation
which if it could work…
                    …might

                                                  ... and
                                                  ... and
                                                  ... am
standing rarely standing high
thinking rarely thinking much
believing rarely believing at all

numbness devours as ages of disbelief
        disrupt sentimentality
the sensitivity to it
        sensibility
        awareness
reinforcing irreverence
           irresponsibility
        apathy
questioning conflicts
        for this is not submission
                          but confusion
question the constitutionality of continuity
        ethics
        capability

... if
unveiling one shaven glimpse
one silver sliver of the eclipsed moon
... if
this could make it all
mean something?

Again and Again

                    the blues is guts and pain
              it's the rawness that come
      from singin' this song
again and again

Catherine Maia Santamaria

Universal Voice

She was a woman with a universal voice.
It was her own voice, born of the world,
and borne by the singing wind.

The low timbre haunted, echoed,
entered the soul.
The cadence underscored and punctuated
the truthful content of her words.

Sometimes spoken softly,
sometimes loudly, shaking in their accuracy,
sometimes overflowing,

'til her lips and tongue stumbled,
stuttering in earnest anxiousness,
to convey her inner voice.

Velvet Black

from virgin sunrises
    to junkie sunsets

roseate dawns
    explosive noons
    beautiful dreams fading in twilight
        to velvet black

how often have I sung this refrain
for some dear friend of mine?
        and now for you
        oh my God
        now it's you this time.

Catherine Maia Santamaria

Last Year

Spring storms
destroyed youth and
scattered friends, leaving ends.

Summer
though warm, lacked heat,
and yielded no harvest.

Fall left
its dry leaves of
grave illness and sorrow
rattling anxiously
in the forest.

Winter
brought cold rains of
quinine, and
a hibernation of white
silence.

Exegesis

Random variations
     of words
form intriguing configurations
  on any blank space,
providing amusement and assurance
    for those who wonder.

Re-examining
 these volutes
 and finding crystal patterns
pacifies,
 aligning the curious
    toward infinity.

But upon re-evaluation
 one becomes aware
of minds
  unexercised in consideration.

Yet, even acknowledgment of
  the gossamer threads
    still does not absolve one.

For there is still a necessity
    to recognize the commission
        of an invitation.

Catherine Maia Santamaria

Thunder with the Snow

You get the thunder with the snow
from the sky and down the mountain.
Get the splendor with the snow.
Get the terror with the snow.
You get the whole show
with love.

Heart beat heat and soul sleet.
The lightning slices up the night
in jagged pieces
of mosaic dark and white.
You get the whole show
with love.

You get the sun with the snow.
Get the afterglow.
Get the rainbow.
You get the whole show
with love.

You can feel the awe.
Step outside
and sink in up to your knees.
Down on your knees.
Free fall to make angels in the snow.
You get it all
with love.

Spring
Singing with Winged Birds

May's Lament

I wore my love heart yesterday
    bright and gold in my hair
there for any to take away
    and keep or break or share.

I think today as no one nears
    I'll tuck it in a nest
with childhood dreams of golden years
    deep in my dowry chest.

So there I was alone and free
    and surely you did smile!
Yet who then said it might be "we?"
    and who was full of guile?

I shall unpack my heart in May
    from mothballs and covers
and let it free: it would not stray
    If you and I were lovers.

But April rains and reigns with you
    May has no time to bloom.
For April stays and lays with you.
    O'er May she casts her gloom.

Catherine Maia Santamaria

I'll wear my heart to lure the sun
      perhaps a rose or two
and I'll wait 'til summer come
        for days of golden hue.

Alas! I've gone from spring to summer's light
But for you, 'tis always April, e'en tonight.

Wander Down the Road

I've been wandering down just any road
for such a long, long time.
Walking wherever there seemed to be
somewhere to go or something new.

Never bothered much with who was by my side.
Usually it was just a helping hand,
and if someone crossed my mind
I'd let them cross the road too.

Never felt trouble much
except when the wind wouldn't blow.
Then I'd stand like a frightened bird
and tremble till I remembered my song.

Traveling alone from night to day
always seemed the best to do.
Never meant to move over
but now, damn, there's you.

Catherine Maia Santamaria

Sun Bluems

Sun bluems
spill in glory
o'er their pot with a sudden spot
of vermillion.

Today

i

  the clear waters are so broken
there is no reflection
    of the waving light:
no mirror
  of our imaginations.
the opaline sea that shimmered, shivers,
and shatters into sharp shards of discontent.
splintered light glances off the surface,
   diverted by dust,
and forms entangled cobweb patterns
   that reflect the steel stars in the sky,
silver slivers crossing and recrossing
   forming a cross
in the deep blue-black velvet space.

ii

the wind is tangled in the branches of growth:
        caught in life,
        caught in love.
called away from freedom, and
   entwined, not by the old and gnarled,
   but by the young and green.
sighing, misting, crying, wishing
   it could be caught into a patterned sphere,
but knowing of the longing and the mourning for the

Catherine Maia Santamaria

lost freedom, last freedom, lasting freedom...
it struggles, crying, changing, laughing.

iii

the heat has forged some new metal
  with rough orange untried unshod edges.
sparking with a white-red light
  that touches awe and fear,
the embers of the embryo glow
giving incandescent flame and blue confusion,
  yet still a creation,
carved and molten
  in its majesty
and the fire leaves ashes and flashes
  of flame that form
    swiftly flickering patterns on the wall:
  knitting and skittering,
  slinking like a tiger cub at play.

iv

the beige earth is rooted deep
  and often it seems wan and cold,
 but it is merely strong and old.
it has been molded mightily,
  heaving in its grey disquiet,
producing voluminous volutes,
  voluptuous in its grandeur.
and though it has long been
  scarred and charred and scourged,

raped and reamed and reaped,
it will go on revolving
  in its constantly dissolving
    continually evolving patterns.

:||

faith is often
  dampened
  worn away
  charred
  buried.

walking, I see the patterns
        formation, life, growth, evolution
watching, I see them weave
        crossing, entwining, knitting, combining
waking, I will not leave
        light, freedom, love, continuity…

Catherine Maia Santamaria

Silent Shadows

Silent
shadows of ghosts,
clouds gather overhead.
Somewhere silence slips softly by.
Grey cat.

All the Smiles

All the smiles
on all the faces of the clouds
pale to white from grey
and entice your love to show
in colours
dwindling after the noon
glancing off
the rocks and shadows
the moss grows soft and cool
for your head to nestle
in the leaves and the grass
the blades to bend and blending in
'til the sun sheds the day
and an evening
of sunstreaks and moonstreams
with yellow silver and
tangerine umber gleams
and lingers on your
contemplative face.

Catherine Maia Santamaria

Loving Stranger

Loving stranger
    when I meet you
I feel so alone.

As I stare into your eyes
    they mirror my surprise
        at seeing parts of me I've never known.

I thought I was so whole without knowing you.
    Yet meeting you
I become translucent,
    an amorphous cloud
        that I cannot contain
            or define or explain.

I've heard it said
    that love is blind.
Do you mind
    if I agree
only part of the time?

I've heard it said
        that one cannot tell
a sunrise from a sunset
        merely by looking at the colours.

Are these flowers
    for me to adorn
        or to mourn with?

Balance!

Poised on
 a pinion,
the eagle dares to slice the wind and
       plummet towards the rocks,
pivoting at that infinitesimal instant
          before infinity.

But the elusive doe of expectation
      will dart,
      fleet foot away,
at the slightest twinge of an atom of its being.

While ballerinas twirl on taut toes,
      and pose en pointe.

         Balance!

Catherine Maia Santamaria

April 22ⁿᵈ at the Symphony

Silence. Darkness.
A faint outline, a silhouette,
    of a boy with dark hair,
    wearing a dark suit,
    sitting in the dark,
    a row in front of me.

Lights! The applause!
Startling, in brilliant red, a younger boy
is on the stage, playing Chopin.
It is flawless, precise, exquisite.
I can see the critics' reviews.

But then slowly invading, persistent,
I hear another piano, proud, almost defiant,
the boy sitting in the dark is silently playing.
I can see his hands in the dark
passionate, unrestrained, glorious.

Chopin comes again, meticulous, beautiful.
We applaud, breaking the thin shell of the classic,
shattering it into shards rudely to pay homage.
We stand and laugh, nervous:
we go home to cry later.

Backstage.
Where is he? We want him!
Swarm around the small shy boy.
How small he is! How brilliant!

Standing near,
arm protectively around his brother,
the boy I heard playing in my memory.

Catherine Maia Santamaria

Listen to the Blues Done Right

the blues at night
gives your mind a place to go

the blues sung right
kicks your troubles out the door

the blues done right
cleans your heart and soul

Love Circled

love
    circled like a dog
        mad blind and hungry
            taking all it could
                leaving me angry
                    then it ran...

love
    circled like a gull
        slow and lazy
            cradling me in a lull
                soft and hazy
                    then it glided...

love
    arrived as a child
        curious and thoughtless
            awkward and changing
                and I was helpless
                    once it left...

love
    circled like the moon
        captivating me
            with the ocean's
                ebb and flow
                  enrapturing me
                    then it waned...

Catherine Maia Santamaria

love
> circled like the seasons
>> consistent in its changing,
>>> renewing and reassuring,
>>>> then it curled up around us
>>> content
>>>> and stayed.

Whistle Bird

Whistle bird
perched on
my window sill
whither fly?
Towards limpid rose
lying on
mahogany table?
But dust moth
flies to lamp,
dies and dries
by wilt rose.
So whistle bird
whither fly?
Find blue white
skies
and soar on
silver rainbows.

Catherine Maia Santamaria

Hot Sunlight

The clarion tones of birds and children
    are amply strewn by the zephyrs.
Stirred by the breezes,
    the jade and emerald trees shake,
sending showers of sunsplashes
shining, shimmering, through the shadows.
Hyacinths, mimosas, and wild raspberries
replace the bitter gall of winter.
Spring heat seeps through me with the
    purity and sureness of warm amber molasses.
And the sun lingers like my lover,
    filling me with light.

Exist

walk by the sea
    salt sea
and speak no loud questions
    simply softly sandily
        exist

    for a while
walk by the sea
    salt sea
feel the seeping sand under your feet
    gaze at the deep murky green
        white foam
  listen quietly
        to gulls and waves calling
  breathe the sharp salt air
easily

    and flow beyond
merely
    slowly
    only for a while
walk by the sea
    salt sea
and
    exist

Catherine Maia Santamaria

www.ingramcontent.com/pod-product-compliance
Lightning Source LLC
LaVergne TN
LVHW010319070426
835512LV00028B/3493